Art o

A pocket guide to r

E quindi uscimmo a riveder le stelle.

And so we came forth, and once again
beheld the stars.

Dante

Peter Hill

First published by Speak Up Somerset in 2005
on behalf of South Somerset Mind
This second edition published 2006

Author: Simon Heyes
Editor: Stephen Tate

South Somerset Mind
The Markwick Centre
Dampier Street
Yeovil BA21 4EN
01935 474875
www.southsomersetmind.co.uk

Speak Up Somerset
PO Box 3484
Yeovil
BA21 5ZH
01935 850979
www.artofrecovery.com

Printers: Character Graphics 01823 279009
ISBN 0-9549772-1-1

South Somerset Mind

AWARDS
FOR ALL

Art of Recovery

Introduction 4

What is recovery? 7

I. Inactive 8
II. Reactive 22
III. Creative 36
IV. Relapse 48

Conclusion 54

Selected bibliography 56

Acknowledgments
Special thanks to: Peter Hill, manager of South Somerset Mind for his vision; Deirdre Seyburn, Astri Griffin, and Jennifer Baxani for their honesty; consultant psychiatrist Glenn Roberts for his inspiration; Aaron Rotheram and Diane Brodie for their illustrations; Jan Wallcraft, Richard Moore, Norman Webley, David Dixon, Jon Gilbert and Maureen Street for their invaluable help; and the staff at Summerlands Hospital site for starting me on the road to recovery.

"Until one is committed, there is hesitancy, the chance to draw back, always ineffectiveness. Concerning all acts of initiative and creation, there is one elementary truth, the ignorance of which kills countless ideas and splendid plans: that the moment one definitely commits oneself, then providence moves too. All sorts of things occur to help one that would never otherwise have occurred. A whole stream of events issues from the decision, raising in one's favour all manner of unforeseen incidents and meetings and material assistance, which no man could have dreamed would have come his way. Whatever you do, or dream you can, begin it. Boldness has genius, power and magic in it. Begin it now."

Johann Wolfgang von Goethe

I have written this guide to recovering from mental distress from the perspective of someone who has had two mental breakdowns. I want to share my experience as well as the experiences of others, who overcome similar obstacles and turned their lives round. The collective aim is to offer a path back to leading a full and meaningful life again.

For too long, society has hidden away those who fall prey to mental health problems. Cast to the fringes, we languish in the shadows bearing an uncomfortable truth that society does not want to acknowledge. We are not the only ones that feel disaffected with the endemic pressures of modern life. Many do but they have found a strategy for coping, be it alcohol, friends, or going on holiday. Meanwhile, they ostracise those who struggle to cope with larger versions of the same problem.

There was a time when I felt I was the only one who didn't fit in but then I looked about me and saw many in a similar position. People with mental health problems have been described as the soul or conscience of society. I think that our mental collapses may be indicative of deeper faultlines within society. If society recognised their universal relevance then our voyages of recovery could offer beacons of hope and we, as a result, might feel more included.

My experience tells me that recovery is a realistic goal. It does not mean I am cured. I sense I will always have what novelist C P Snow describes in *The Light and the Dark* as "the special melancholy which belongs to some chosen natures". Part of my recovery was realising that this melancholy came from the same source as my strengths. I cannot have one without the other.

Art of Recovery is about taking steps to regain your place in the world. To cultivate an unshakeable belief that you are still a contender in this thing called life and to focus on your well-being, your strengths and what you have to offer. Two steps begin the recovery process. The first is to believe that it is possible to recover. The second is to be realistic. There are no quick fixes. Recovery is not a straight line from unwell to well but I am convinced that once lost, mental well-being is retrievable.

If you would like to join the increasing number of people who believe that recovery is a possibility, please send in thoughts, advice and personal accounts of recovery that others might find helpful. I wrote *Art of Recovery* in the hope that it provides inspiration that you can recover.

Aaron Rotheram

Recovery is not about finding a miracle cure or returning to how things used to be. It is about finding a better, healthier and more sustainable life that recognises the past, accepts the limitations of the present and is full of hope for the future. I have experienced the downside of searching for the quick fix; life is more complicated than the trite solutions peddled in self-help books. This guide aims to stimulate the power within us all to climb up our own ladder of recovery.

Stages of recovery

I have separated the recovery process into three stages. The first stage is called the inactive stage. This is when you have broken down and can no longer function. The second is the reactive stage. This is the point when you begin to look for ways to re-engage with life. The third is the creative stage. This is when you take charge of your life. You have turned things round and have established a cycle of behaviour that looks after your well-being. I refer to this as a recovery syndrome but don't be put off. I see this syndrome as something that is good for you.

The following lists of words should help you identify with the different stages:

Inactive	Reactive	Creative
Hiding	Running	Opening
Empty	Restless	Fulfilled
Controlled	Controlling	Allowing
Losing	Fighting	Winning
Overloaded	Passive	Pro-active
Nothing	Receiving	Giving
Locked	Unlocked	Open
Numb	Serious	Fun
Shock	Anger	Acceptance
Dark	Grey	Light

"For those who have dwelt in depression's dark wood and known its inexplicable agony, their return from the abyss is not unlike the ascent of the poet trudging upward and upward out of hell's black depths and at last emerging into what he saw as 'the shining world'."

William Styron

Peter Hill

"When you get low in spirit and discouraged, remember this:
The lowest ebb is the turn of the tide."

Henry Wadsworth Longfellow

Inactive

"He now watched his good reputation sink step by step in his teacher's eyes, from good to fair, from fair to satisfactory, satisfactory to unsatisfactory...No-one could penetrate the desperate smile on the boy's small face to the foundering spirit within, suffering and looking about him in terror and despair as he sank."

Hermann Hesse

I had my first breakdown in 1988, when I was twenty-three. I was in Australia on a working holiday and playing rugby in my spare time. I felt out of sorts to begin with. Then came a creeping sense of unease which I couldn't shake off. I could not sleep. I lost all sense of fun or vitality. I became preoccupied with the past, lost interest in the present and saw no hope for the future. I was consumed by negative emotions of guilt and panic. My consciousness had altered from relatively normal to troubled, which left me feeling disorientated.

Deep down, I hoped for a miracle. Something to bring back my old self. But my distress only grew. It became so intense I could hardly function. Why couldn't I pull myself together? I asked myself this question countless times but I had no answer. I could cope with rugby, people and work but not my mind. Nothing had prepared me for this experience. I went to see a doctor who gave me some pills. I took them all at once and my flat mates found me the next day. They took me to hospital where I was injected with a high dose of medication to calm me down. Within hours I had been admitted to a psychiatric hospital. The first thing I remember clearly is waking up miles from home, feeling tormented. I had broken down in mind and spirit but I tried to blot out what was happening. I refused to accept that I had been admitted to a psychiatric hospital. I wanted to keep my identity intact at any cost.

I returned to England with my confidence in tatters. The thought of social interaction was daunting enough, let alone talking about what had happened in Australia. I felt embarrassed about what had happened and the stigma attached to being mentally unwell made me want to hide away. I only discovered later that people around me had experienced similar suffering. One of my cousins had been diagnosed with manic depression. Mental distress had also cast a shadow over members of my local rugby club, fellow school pupils and friends of the family. We shared a common sense of shame, which left us feeling isolated.

I put my problems on hold in the hope that one day they might disappear of their own accord. That day never came and seven years later, I had another breakdown. I was about to qualify as a general nurse at a hospital in Cheshire. Once again I ended up in psychiatric care.

For two years, all I wanted to do was to stay in bed curled up in the foetal position facing the wall. I was unable to find any joy in life and saw no light at the end of the tunnel. I received medication and counselling and eventually underwent electric shock therapy. On reflection, my breakdowns did not happen out of the blue. The warning signs had been around for some time. I had been an anxious child, uncertain of myself. I had struggled to live up to the expectations that I had set myself. I suffered from phobias and spent most of my teenage years convinced that I had cancer.

Feeling mentally unwell is like having someone place a heavy weight on your mind and soul. The pressure is unbearable. You feel alone. You dwell on past mistakes. You don't sleep. You believe that you will never get better. I have never forgotten this stage. Mental health professionals use clinical language to classify the symptoms of mental illness. It gives them an objective framework to work within. But those who experience mental distress need more powerful ways to describe what they are going through. Evocative phrases such as 'cancer of the soul', 'malignant sadness' and Winston Churchill's famous 'black dog' bring personal meaning to our condition. They sum up how we feel in ways that psychiatric labels never will.

William Styron suggests in *Darkness Visible* that a fellowship exists between people who have experienced mental collapse. We have been to a fearful place and made it back. Though our individual stories are different, we share a like mind. Recovery is about recognising the common threads that link you to others.

Case history

Deirdre Seyburn had a breakdown after two previous suicide attempts. She was forty and diagnosed with depression and a personality disorder. She used to be a choreographer, line dance instructor and freelance journalist but now works as a mental health volunteer. She is forty-five and lives in Gloucestershire.

"The balance had never been quite right in my life. I was the sort of person who couldn't say no. I lived life at a 100 miles per hour and never stopped to wonder about the emotional cost. With two previous suicide attempts behind me, I was bound to crash again.

I was self-employed and doing what seemed like three people's jobs at once. Burn out crept up on me slowly over a period of about three years. My behaviour changed. My head felt like it was going to explode. I drank heavily to numb the pain. I didn't eat for days, then I binged. My weight ballooned to 18 stone. I told

Diane Brodie

myself I was still 10 stone. I wouldn't accept how poorly I had become. I portrayed an outward image that said all was okay, whereas inside I was dying. It was only when someone wrote down my weight on a piece of paper that I woke up to reality. I felt so ashamed that I avoided everyone and everything. I even travelled 30 miles to get my hair cut because I didn't want to bump into people who knew me. I was paranoid, anxious and suffered panic attacks. I lived in a thick, black fog. I didn't want to be here. I wanted out.

They say when the student is ready the teacher will appear and the key to my recovery was a psychiatric nurse called Ken. In our weekly sessions he would challenge my thoughts and behaviour. He made me find out who I really was and what made me tick. Ken was the first person who gave me any hope. He said he wanted to move me forward. I had not heard anyone say those words to me before. I needed someone to believe in me because I had lost my own self-belief.

I became a volunteer at the local Citizens Advice Bureau. It got me out of the house and mixing socially. I also joined a women's only gym and lost two thirds of the weight I had put on. A friend encouraged me to do *reiki* which helped soothe my anxiety.

Looking back, my breakdown was the best thing that ever happened to me. I see it as a breakthrough not a breakdown. I used to take a lot for granted. Now I value simple pleasures like appreciating a flower's beauty. I treat my mental distress as a friend rather than an enemy. I have taken control of my life again."

Inactive tips

1. Trust in you

Our minds can become over-stimulated. Thoughts race through our heads. They jostle, collide and confuse until we lose focus. The act of buying food can seem like a terrible ordeal. This is the point to put faith in your body. It will find its natural balance over time. Trust in its sixth sense to pull you out of the situation.

The healing process has to start somewhere. It will invariably begin when you feel at your lowest ebb; the point when you withdraw into yourself. Psychologist Oliver Sacks uses the term 'vegetative retreat' and I feel this accurately describes the point when you reach rock bottom. There are compensations for arriving here. It is the moment to face unresolved issues and identify the pressures that have dragged you down. This will give you an opportunity to relieve those pressures and work towards reconnecting with a life of meaning and purpose.

2. Take good care of yourself

A doctor once told me that people who are mentally unwell often neglect their teeth and feet. I know from experience that looking after your appearance seems like an unnecessary chore when you are feeling low. Force yourself. It will encourage you to feel that all is not lost.

Positive Role Model - Athlete Kelly Holmes is famous for winning two gold medals at the 2004 Olympic Games in Athens. Afterwards, she admitted that she had self-injured herself prior to the games because she was in such despair.

Focus on your body's basic needs. Get enough rest because lack of sleep amplifies your mental distress. Take exercise. A daily walk will do the power of good. And eat healthy foods, which will provide your body with vitamins and minerals.

3. Distress Benefits

Giving up my career in nursing was a painful decision to take. Perhaps my breakdown was my mind's way of telling me that the path I had chosen was not for me. Evolutionary psychologist Randolph Nesse believes that depression acts as a check on people who set themselves unrealistic targets. It forces them to disconnect from their unwinnable quest. Dr Tim Cantopher refers to depression as "the curse of the strong". He believes that people who push themselves to the limit are more prone to mental breakdown, writing that "it's always the best ones who get ill." I pushed myself beyond my abilities. Perhaps my breakdowns were the only mechanism that my body could use to rein in my persistent nature.

4. Love me tender

The last thing you want to hear is pull yourself together. If it was that easy, you would have done it a long time ago. What you need is someone there for you. A non-judgmental companion who will offer gentle affection, make cups of tea, take long walks and most importantly, listen. For me, it was my sister who provided the companionship that I needed. After my first breakdown, she came out to Australia, visited me in hospital and flew home with me. A friend also visited and gave me a compilation of my favourite music.

"Sometimes our light goes out but it is blown into flame by an encounter with another human being. Each of us owes the deepest thanks to those who have rekindled this inner light."

Albert Schweitzer

In his book, T*he Noonday Demon: An Atlas of Depression*, Andrew Solomon recommends that family and friends should try and blunt the isolation of the mentally unwell. Express how you feel to your family and friends. They will invariably want to understand why you feel so low, even if they find the process difficult. Nurture this support because they are the ones who want you to recover the most.

5. One step at a time

"Get up, stay up and go to bed" are three tasks one friend sets himself when he lapses into deep depression. It makes him feel that he has still made something of his day. My sister used to say to me when I was in hospital: "Take baby steps." Your recovery will be easier to swallow if you break it down into bite-size chunks. Try and strike a balance between doing too much and doing too little. Rein in your expectations and congratulate yourself on those small victories, like getting out of bed in the morning.

6. Be realistically unwell

Once upon a time, a depressed man went to see a doctor. The doctor advised him to go and see Grimaldi the famous clown to cheer himself up. "I am Grimaldi the famous clown", the man replied. This story shows how regardless of appearances, we all struggle at times to make sense of life. Dr Viktore E Frankl, who survived Auschwitz, believed millions of people bought his book *Man's Search for Meaning,* because it tackled "a question that burns under the fingernails". Some become so preoccupied with the question that it affects their ability to function. Shelley E Taylor argues in *Positive Illusions* that the mentally unwell have a more realistic view of the world. They see through the illusions of life to the clear light of reality. Winston Churchill wrote of his depression: "Why do I get stuck down in the past? Why do I keep going over and over those years when I know that I cannot change anything?" Resist the urge to exaggerate the significance of bad days. You will have good days, too, and these should be celebrated.

7. Recognise change

"This, too, will pass" is a favourite phrase of newspaper agony aunt Virginia Ironside, who suffered long bouts of depression. The saying is believed to come from the reign of King Solomon. It is said the monarch ordered his court philosopher to come up with an inscription for a sun dial in the royal gardens. The king set two conditions: the inscription had to apply to any hour of the day; and its meaning had to be the same whether the king felt wonderfully happy or unutterably sad. The philosopher pondered the riddle for many hours then returned to the king with four words: "This, too, will pass."

8. Beware of false friends

Cigarettes and alcohol are not great company in times of distress. Smoking is one of the leading causes of lung cancer and heart disease. Excessive drinking increases anxiety and damages the liver irreparably. Caffeine is another one to avoid. Too much tea and coffee activates your adrenal glands, which increases stress levels.

Beware of the self-help industry as well. I used to be an avid reader of self-help books. I was convinced that they would give me the answers to my problems. I am not alone. Americans spend an estimated four billion pounds on self-help products every year. The industry has mushroomed in the past decade, with books, courses, seminars, videos, CDs and DVDs offering formulas and miracles to lost souls desperate for answers. A far cry from the age of Samuel Smiles, who wrote the first best-selling self-help book as long ago as 1859.

Self-help gurus use neat formulas that gloss over the complexities of life. The end result can often leave you feeling a failure because the promised magic has not worked. David Burnet's *Sects, Cults and Alternative Religions* devotes a whole chapter to the self-help phenomenon. He argues that a cult of "personal development" has filled the vacuum left by the decline of political ideologies like Marxism and Communism.

Maybe there is no magic wand that will suddenly make your life wonderful. Instead of being habitually disappointed by the empty promises made by the self-help industry, learn to trust your own intuition. It wants to help not make money from your misery. If the dissatisfied voices were heard collectively, we might reduce the predatory instincts of the self-help age and concentrate on seeking ways to achieve greater success for all.

9. Live in the present

When depressed we become bogged down with regrets about the past. In retrospect there is much we should have done differently but do we know anybody who wouldn't want to change the past? Similarly, our mind can play tricks on us about the future. It can tell us that there is nothing but bad events ahead. Being aware of the present is the goal of mindfulness, central to Buddhist teachings, but anyone can benefit from living more in the present. As the Alcoholics Anonymous saying goes: "It is not the experience of today that drives me mad, it is the remorse of bitterness for something which happened yesterday and the dread of what tomorrow may bring. Let us, therefore, live one day at a time."

10. Hope eternal

Greek mythology tells us that Zeus gave the first mortal woman a box and told her not to open it. Her name was Pandora and the box contained every blessing and every curse ever bestowed upon humanity. As she opened the box, the curses flew out into the world. The blessings left, too, except for one. Hope remained.

Dr Jerome Groopman, author of *The Anatomy of Hope*, argues that hope has a scientific basis: "True hope is clear-eyed. It sees all the difficulties and all the potential for failure but through that, carves a realistic path to a better future." Without hope, we could not endure the trials of life.

Peter Hill

"The most beautiful people are those who have known defeat, known suffering, known struggle, known loss, and have found their way out of the depths. These persons have an appreciation, a sensitivity and an understanding of life that fills them with compassion, gentleness, and a deep loving concern."

Elisabeth Kubler-Ross

"Life begins on the other side of despair."

Jean Paul Satre

Suicidal thoughts

Life can lose its point. Anyone who has had depression will know the feeling. Left unchecked, it can lead to suicidal thoughts. For many, suicide is considered a taboo.Perhaps this unwillingness to engage with the subject arises from a fear of encouraging a deeper introspection that could spiral out of control.

I decided to tackle the question of why live head on and sought guidance from literature. I found solace in Leo Tolstoy's autobiographical *A Confession*, George Eliot's *Daniel Deronda,* Daphne Du Maurier's *I Will Never Be Young Again* and Albert Camus's *The Myth of Sisyphus*. Camus later said of his work: "It sums itself up for me as a lucid invitation to live and to create, in the very midst of the desert." In *Daniel Deronda*, Eliot describes the joyous turning point when Mirah finds hope as she is about to commit suicide: "Goodness came to me living and I trust in the living".

In each book, I met characters who had stepped back from the brink. To the question, is life worth living?, they answered yes. This helped light up a path out of the darkness and put my trust back in the living.

"Sweet are the uses of adversity,
Which like the toad, ugly and venous,
Wears yet a precious jewel in his head."

William Shakespeare

Simon Heyes

"We must accept finite disappointment, but we must never lose infinite hope."

Martin Luther King, Jr.

Reactive

"He suddenly hears himself talking and because he'd been silenced for so long, he'd forgotten that he had ideas and that he was worth more than just an automaton, and it's a wonderful moment of discovery."

Emile Zola

My breakdowns forced me to withdraw from society but there were compensations. It gave me time to ponder, to look, to idle and to think. But eventually, I had to venture out again. Recovery is like learning a new skill. And with any new skill, it takes time to become proficient. My first attempts were like wild swings of my arms but the more I applied myself, the better I became.

My first wild swing was to unicycle from John O'Groats to Land's End in 1998. I felt like a latter day Don Quixote, still in the grips of madness, but grasping at something that I hoped would lift me out of my depression. I felt angry at the way my life had panned out. I was a grown-up. But one with a mental health problem. I needed to channel my frustration and this outlandish trip seemed like the answer. My quest was to break down the stigma surrounding mental health. A man on a unicycle was maybe not the perfect vehicle to launch my cause but I felt inspired. Anyway, it was not the time to be rational. I had to reconnect with the world and the trip flushed me out me into the open in more ways than one. It made me admit to myself that I had been unwell, which dissipated the burning angst inside me. It renewed my confidence.

The unicycle trip took me about a month. I met many interesting people along the way, who gave me lots of encouragement. On my return to Somerset, I helped set up a support group for people who had been through similar experiences. We called it Speak Up Somerset and it thrives to this day. I also wanted to work again. Oxfam took me on as a volunteer, then I became a taxi driver. When not driving a cab, I studied an Open University course in mental health. Passing the course helped assuage my frustration at failing to get my nursing qualification. I also took a diploma in computing. My studies led to a paid job with the NHS, working in the mental health sector. I had turned my life around by reacting to my breakdown and transforming the experience into a positive outcome.

Many good things can come out of a breakdown. Dr Kay Redfield Jamison experienced manic depression first hand. In her book, *An Unquiet Mind*, she writes: "I have felt more things, more deeply; had more experiences, more intensely; loved more and been more loved."

"To live is not just to survive, but to thrive with passion, compassion, some humour and style."

Maya Angelou

Beneficial breakdowns

Bill O'Hanlon's *Thriving Through Crisis* lists the following benefits of a breakdown:

1. Enhanced closeness to others
2. Changed priorities.
3. Increased sensitivity and empathy for others.
4. Increased sense of spirituality.
5. Greater concern with world issues.

Positive Role Model

Winston Churchill suffered from depression. Early on in his political career, he resigned from government following the debacle at Gallipoli in 1915. "I thought he would die of grief," his wife Clementine said. Yet he became a war prime minister and was re-elected prime minister at the age of seventy-six.

Psychiatrist Anthony Storr wrote of Churchill: "Had he been a stable and equable man, he could never have inspired the nation. In 1940, when all the odds were against Britain, a leader of sober judgment might well have concluded that we were finished."

Peter Hill

Case history

Astri Griffin had a breakdown after the birth of her first child. She was twenty-seven and diagnosed with schizophrenia. Three years later, she had a second child. Over the following decade, she had two more breakdowns. She is fifty-six and lives in Somerset.

"When I was bringing up my two children, I accepted my diagnosis thinking I was alone in my suffering. I felt inadequate compared to the ordinary mums I met or saw at playgroups, clubs, the supermarket. Although I tried to act normal, I felt inadequate. Once other mums knew about my illness they dropped me as a friend. A few stayed by me but on the whole I was ostracised. It left me feeling isolated and an oddball.

The turning point came in my early forties when I saw a meeting advertised in the local paper, which invited people with mental health problems to come and share their experiences with others. It was a revelation to find that there were others just like me who were going through similar situations. The realisation that I was not alone was an extraordinary relief. Wow! I thought. I started to help produce a newsletter for a local mental health organisation. The chance to work with like-minded people and the support that we gave each other marked the beginning of my real recovery.

I have always been creative. I used to write and paint but after my first breakdown, I lost my creativity. I devoted myself to bringing up my children at the expense of my own well-being. I know every mother goes through this but in my case I felt like I had disappeared. I was non-existent.

Joining the newsletter released a rush of creative energy, which was fuelled at first by anger and frustration. I drew satirical cartoons, which criticised the mental health system. I also wrote articles offering alternative theories on dealing with mental health. It was a productive phase.

As the anger dissipated, I was able to start work again on my art and writing as an artist and as a writer, rather than as someone who was mentally ill. I am an artist first who has experienced mental health problems rather a mentally ill person who paints."

Astri Griffin

Reactive tips

1. Be comfortable with being uncomfortable

Certain times, certain places, certain events or anniversaries will trigger feelings of loneliness, emptiness and depression. It's okay to feel like this. It doesn't mean that you're ill. Everyone has times and places that make them feel uncomfortable. Some of us feel nervous in smart places, others in dingy places, while beautiful people make us all nervous! Eleanor Roosevelt once said: "No-one can make you feel inferior without your consent." Be yourself. Express yourself. Celebrate who you are. Eventually, you will find your own level.

2. Pause to think

Remember you are making progress when you feel depressed. It shows you have feelings. In my case, I saw it as a step up from the absence of feelings that I experienced after my breakdowns. Andrew Solomon's *The Noonday Demon: An Atlas of Depression* argues that depression contains "seeds of self-examination" that begin a process which is "usually fruitful".

Once beyond the stage of sustenance, you will have the opportunity to use your depression as a catalyst for change. In *Productive and Unproductive Depression*, Emmy Gut suggests that depression forces us to pause. These pauses give us time to reflect on our lives. The process can lay the groundwork on which to make positive changes later on. This is a golden opportunity to become the architect of your own recovery. So be wary not to squander the chance by dwelling on past mistakes. Change your thinking around and profit from failure. As Australian cricket legend Greg Chapple once said: "All the successful people I know have failed."

3. The peeler state

Mental distress takes a physical toll. Tiredness often seems to go hand in hand with being mentally unwell because our biological rhythms are so out of sync. It feels like living with permanent jet lag, forever out of kilter with the cycle of everyday life. Even if the worst of our mental distress ends, because our regular waking and sleeping patterns are disrupted subtle negative thinking patterns seem to make us liable to slip into depression. Be wary of this circadian 'jet lag'. Conserve your energy and use it wisely. Some days will be more productive than others. You will get loads done one day then struggle to get through another. Know your limitations and let family and friends know them, too.

Psychiatrist Glenn Roberts uses the metaphor of the peeler stage of the life cycle of a crab to illustrate how we need to face vulnerability to mature. During the peeler stage the crab sheds it shell as it grows bigger, leaving it defenceless while a new shell forms. During this stage the crab grows towards maturity but faces danger. I like this metaphor and believe during recovery we may feel exposed but this opens us up to change. Only then can we build new and stronger defences.

4. Find the off switch

According to Dr Tim Cantopher, people who suffer from depression become ill because they are strong. They share common character traits, including moral fortitude, reliability, a strong sense of right and wrong and the will to help others before themselves. They can also be sensitive and vulnerable to criticism. All these qualities can be perceived as strengths rather than weaknesses. The danger is to go beyond the point when the warning signs tell us to stop. When we over-reach ourselves and suffer the fallout. Managed sensibly, your strengths have enormous potential to make a positive difference to your life and the lives of those around you.

5. Kick down the statues

How you feel may not be all your own doing. I think too much emphasis is placed on personal and psychological factors to explain mental disorders. Political and philosophical factors shape our lives, too, so neglecting their effect on our mental health seems a blinkered approach to me. Society is in constant flux. Values change, doctrines change. These shifts in popular thinking impact on our lives for better, or worse. They belong in the equation that determines why we feel the way we do.

Instigate change. Channel your anger into making a difference. Target barriers to recovery from mental distress; be it government policy, lack of work opportunities, racism, poverty, or the stigma attached to being mentally unwell. Join action groups. Become informed. Campaign for change. Say what makes you feel angry. Be proactive. Feel involved rather than helpless.

6. Keep it real

In Arthur Miller's *Death of a Salesman*, the main character Willy Loman lives under the illusion that he is destined for success. He can only cope with his failures by living in the past. As a result, he loses touch with reality. American satirist James Thurber explores a similar theme in *The Secret Life of Walter Mitty*. Mitty is a meek and hen-pecked husband who daydreams of being a heroic fighter pilot, or a dashing naval commander, to escape the monotony of his mundane life: "Throw on the power lights! Rev her up to 8500! We're going through!" he declares. We can all identify with Walter Mitty's desire to live the dream but how many of us can admit to having a colourful inner life. Maybe you dream of winning the lottery, or flying through space. We all do it.

Depression feeds on self doubt. It can convince you that everyone fits in except you. Stanley Cohen and Laurie Taylor's reveal in *Escape Attempts from Everyday Life* how close to madness are many of our everyday efforts to avoid the reality of life. It helped me realise that I was not unusual; that there were lots of people out there like me who experienced moments of confusion and isolation.

7. Mind the gap

Modern consumer societies pose an intriguing paradox; we are richer, healthier and have more choice than ever before but we don't appear to be any happier. It seems the gap between what we are and what we would like to be is ever widening. In *Paradox of Choice,* Barry Schwartz argues that an excess of choice is at the heart of our discontent. He believes that we have reached a point where choice has become detrimental to our well-being rather than beneficial. The idea that we can choose our own way in life may provide motivation for some to get on but it also leaves many of us tortured by our failure to live up to the goals we set. This idea that we achieve what we want in life is misleading, because by the law of averages not all of can come out on top. We can't all have the most interesting job, or the big house by the sea. Yet in this time of personal choice, we blame ourselves for missing out by making the wrong decisions in our lives. Schwartz writes: "Unobtainable expectations, plus a tendency to take intense personal responsibility for failure, make for a lethal combination." At the same time as being bombarded with choice, we are losing the ballast that keeps our lives afloat; strong family ties, friendly neighbours, loyal friends. Competition for the best jobs has intensified, while the fabled job for life has all but gone. It is no wonder then that many of us feel insecure and push ourselves hard. One of the consolations of having a breakdown is the chance to re-appraise your priorities and to listen to your own heart. It can empower you to re-build a life based on your own values.

8. Negative agendas

You may find that others feel threatened by your positive approach when you start to do something about your recovery. They may try to put you down. Learning to cope with difficult people is an important skill to master. If someone launches a personal attack, try and deflect it with humour, then try and make them aware that their comments were hurtful. Perennially negative people are best avoided.

9. Funny bones

I know someone who used stand-up comedy to overcome acute social anxiety. He struggled to communicate at school and hardly left his room when he was at university but humour has shown him a way out. Each public performance demonstrates his recovery. Hope may well be the most important component of any recovery, but humour runs it pretty close. "A sense of humour is the best indicator that you will recover; it is often the best indicator that people will love you. Sustain that and you have hope," writes Andrew Solomon in *An Atlas of Depression*. Re-framing negative experiences helps us come to terms with them. As Karen Blixen, author of *Out of Africa*, writes: "All sorrows can be borne, if you put them into a story, or tell a story about them".

10. Force of nature

Your doors of perception will change as you begin to recover. One of the great pleasures of my recovery was the moment I felt the beauty of nature like never before. I was on a beach in Devon. The roar of the breaking waves, the smooth sheen of the shoreline as the tide ebbed out; they became marvels of power and light. I saw nature through new eyes. My spirit soared.

Simon Heyes

"Our real blessings often appear to us in the shape of pains, losses and disappointments; but let us have patience, and we shall soon see them in their proper figures."

Joseph Addison

Dealing with loss

Coming to terms with loss is a big challenge in recovery. Loss takes many forms, be it loss of self-confidence, potential, control, self-respect, position in society, a job, a university place, friends, or relationships. In *On Death and Dying,* Dr Elizabeth Kubler-Ross, founder of the hospice movement, proposes that terminally-ill patients move through five stages of grief: denial, anger, bargaining, depression and acceptance. Her work provides a rough framework in which to look at how we handle difficult transitions. Dr Trevor Griffiths has applied Kubler-Ross's work on grieving to the mental health field. In *Lost and Found: Turning Life's Disappointments into Hidden Treasures*, he suggests that patients often experience mental distress because they have not recognised that they are overwhelmed by grief.

I remember almost drowning in a sea of anger, guilt and depression but the tide turned and the current carried me to acceptance. Dr Griffiths describes acceptance as "joy tempered by sadness"; joy in letting go, being more creative, exploring new possibilities and living a full and mature life; and sadness in recognising that we have lost something along the way. Confronting loss courageously can make us stronger, wiser and more compassionate.

Loss has the power to crush us. It can also give us a deeper appreciation of life. Philosopher Nicholas Wolterstorff lost his twenty-five year old son in a climbing accident. In *Lament For A Son*, he describes the solace that helped him come to terms with the loss of his son: "There emerges a radiance which seldom appears elsewhere; a glow of courage, of love, of insight, of selflessness, of faith. In that radiance we see best what humanity was meant to be. In the valley of suffering, despair and bitterness are brewed. But there also character is made."

Life's setbacks can make us more understanding of others, more appreciative of life and more aware of the things that matter most; our health, family and friends. Part of a successful recovery is to grow from our losses and harvest a rosier future.

Stephen Tate

"Sadness flies away on the wings of change."
Jean de la Fontaine

Peter Hill

"Look ahead to the peace of recovery and let time carry you there."

Clare Weekes

"As my suffering mounted, I soon realised that there were two ways in which I could respond to my situation; either to react with bitterness, or seek to transform the suffering into a creative force. I choose the latter."

Martin Luther King

As the sharp edges of my mental breakdown softened, I became aware of the old 'Simon' returning. It was time for me to create a new life rather than simply react against my situation. I was fed up with fighting with myself and the outside world. It was never going to make me feel better. I decided to plough my energy into creating a sustainable recovery. I told myself that I wanted a joyful life like everyone else and I set about making it happen. Writer Lesley Dormen wrote of her depression: "I don't know where my depression comes from or where it goes. I do know that it was the crucible, the rite of passage, that allowed me to create my life."

One book stood out like a beacon of hope. Tim Lott's *The Scent of Dried Roses* is an autobiographical account of his recovery from suicidal depression. It spoke to me far more than any psychiatrist, or self-help manual could. Here was a story I could relate to; someone who had eaten Fruit Pastilles and watched Sergeant Bilko as a child but had experienced panic attacks and depression of such magnitude that he describes the need to commit suicide as "the greatest certainty I have ever known". Despite this, and the suicide of his own mother, he recovered. Lott believes that depression is about the search for identity and our struggle to fit into society. "In finding a solution to identity, you begin to find a solution to depression."

In *The Road Less Travelled,* Dr M Scott Peck describes experiencing acute unhappiness at boarding school. Rather than tread the path of privilege to a good university and the higher echelons of society, Peck left school and was admitted to a psychiatric hospital: "Even if it meant being crazy and out of step with all that seemed holy, I had decided to be me."

I started to find my identity and place in the world by producing a diary featuring artwork done by people affected by mental distress. I also began to play cricket and found the courage to travel again. In 2004, I went round the world to attend a recovery training programme

Positive Role Model John Kirwan, one of the best rugby players that New Zealand has ever produced, suffered from depression for much of his career. He once had a panic attack during an international game against France. Since his retirement, he has worked to promote greater awareness of mental illness. He believes depression has made him a better person.

in the US. The trip gave me an opportunity to go back to Australia, the place I had left ignominiously some sixteen years before. This time, I returned feeling mentally and physically well. It was a cathartic experience, like the unicycle trip across the UK, and as I stood outside the psychiatric clinic in Brisbane, I wondered how many of my fellow patients had also recovered.

The trip had several unexpected bonuses. I overcame a fear of flying and conquered an obsessive compulsive food disorder. I had convinced myself in psychiatric care that I suffered from an extreme peanut allergy. I made a conscious decision to conquer this irrational fear as an air stewardess gave me a bag of peanuts. I ate them without thinking about the consequences. It was a major step in my recovery. I don't think it was simple biology at work. I had reconciled something deep within me and healed the open wound that despair inflicts at these depths. It brought renewal and a creative existence.

Aaron Rotheram

Case History

Peter Hill went to boarding school between the ages of ten and fifteen. He has suffered from depression for most of his life and has survived three suicide attempts. He works full-time in the mental health field. He is fifty-eight, married with three children and lives in Somerset.

"My depression started when I was young. Boarding school was an unhappy experience. I was born with a murmur in my heart, which meant I was not allowed to play contact sports. I could not join in with the other children playing football. I saw myself as an outcast, lonely and isolated. I was also dyslexic. The condition was not really recognised at the time. My teachers thought I was lazy and treated me badly. It was a harsh environment to grow up in. We were never called by our christian names. There was physical and emotional bullying.

I left school with one O level and a rock bottom opinion of myself and my abilities. A succession of dead end jobs and broken relationships followed. I developed a drink problem. I drank every day and never went to bed totally sober. It was my way of dealing with my unhappiness. I found relationships difficult. I first went to see a GP about my depression in my early twenties. He gave me some pills. Twenty-five years later, I still had depression and had been admitted to a psychiatric hospital twice.

My recovery started during an adult training course. I attended a session on counselling and the trainer said something which brought back a lot of stuff from my past. This event seemed to be a turning-point. I went to art college and completed a degree and MA in fine art. I married and had three children. The birth of my first child led me to stop drinking at the age of thirty-four. I could not cope with being a father and having a drink problem. I wanted to be in control, make myself do things, go to work and do photography, even if there seemed little point.

I know depression colours my perception of life. Part of my recovery is about accepting this. Depression fills me with a sense of foreboding about impending disasters that will leave me divorced, jobless and homeless. Yet when I feel better, I see a different reality. I see a father who has raised a family; I see a husband whose wife has stuck by him for twenty-five years; and I see a man who has travelled widely, enjoyed reasonable health, completed a masters and keeps down a responsible job helping others with mental illness. It's then that I can tell myself that I'm okay."

Peter Hill

Creative tips

1. Master planning

Recovery expert Mary-Ellen Copeland recommends drawing up a Wellness Recovery Action Plan (WRAP) to help self-manage your mental distress. The technique involves identifying tools within you, which you can use to cope with difficult times. A Wrap can manage thoughts of panic, for example, by suggesting you talk to a friend, or go for a walk. The plan is written down and gives you a structure to live through uncomfortable moments without feeling in danger. If things do tumble out of control, your Wrap will also include a crisis plan, which you and others can use to put you back on an even keel.

2. Thaw out

Those of us recovering from mental distress are prone to over-personalise everyday events that occur around us. We may blame ourselves, for example, if someone is angry, or assume without good cause that someone has a negative opinion of us. Life is rarely that black and white. The key is to challenge your thinking. Feelings of anger, fear or frustration are not necessarily unhealthy. They are natural emotions, which may encourage you to take positive action. Harvey Jenkins argues in *The Human Side of Human Beings* that humans deep-freeze

Positive Role Model Mathematician John Nash was awarded a Nobel Prize in Economics in 1994 for his contribution to modern economic theory. He had spent the previous three decades in psychiatric care after being diagnosed as a paranoid schizophrenic. The film, *A Beautiful Mind* (2001), is based on his life.

feelings of distress caused by a negative event. When another negative event occurs, they base their reaction on the frozen response rather than resolving the situation in isolation. We can break this pattern of negative thinking by resuscitating our human ability to adapt to new situations.

3. Medicate with care

I know from experience that we all want instant relief from mental distress. Whilst I acknowledge that many people find medication invaluable to their recovery, I think we should be wary of the potential side effects. As well as making us feel better, drugs alter the way we think. I am concerned about becoming reliant on drugs without never having actually dealt with the root causes of the problem. I agree with Andrew Solomon in *The Atlas of Depression*, who advises that medication should be taken "knowingly, deliberately and reflectively".

4. Find community

We depend on each other to survive yet psychiatrist Claire Weekes says people with mental health problems often feel unable to make contact with others: "It is as though they [other people] are in one world and I am in another."

Feelings of isolation are caused by a loss of self-confidence. One way to reduce the isolation is by meeting others who have been through similar crises. An effective support network will help sustain your recovery. Having friends to call when you feel down is a wonderful safety net, which can prevent things from getting worse. But finding those friends is not so easy in practice. You may have lost touch with old friends and may not feel up to making new ones. Be patient and be open about what you have been through. Eventually, you will meet people who respect your honesty.

Books are another community that can provide inspiration during your recovery. Many people have written about living with mental distress. They range from classic texts such as Clifford Beers's *A Mind That Found Itself*, written in 1908, to more contemporary accounts like Kay Redfield Jamison's graphic portrait of manic depression in *An Unquiet Mind*.

5. Turn on, tune in and slow down

Growing up I felt driven to fit in. I wanted to be seen as 'normal'. Even as I struggled with nearly constant panic attacks when I was nearing the end of my nurse training, I thought the answer was to work harder. Yet it all was for no avail. I was not being myself. Artist John Lane wrote: "You are what you are, and there can be no avoidance of this reality, no camouflage in the interests of ambition, status, income, comfort. You are born with a character; it is a gift to be accepted with grace."

It took me two breakdowns to accept this gift. After my second breakdown I decided to question the social and economic assumptions that underpinned my life. I told myself that I couldn't be the only person who felt out of sorts. I searched for alternative ways of living and working that suited me better. I reined in my expectations, accepted that I had a finite reserve of physical and mental energy and discovered the art of pottering. My solution won't suit all but there are many other alternatives out there. The Slow Food Movement, for example, the art of loafing, or simply downshifting to a simpler way of life.

6. Feel better for free

The basics of life are there for everyone to enjoy; a walk in a park, marvelling at the night sky, cooking a meal, writing a letter, talking to a friend, reading a book, getting into a freshly-made bed. Take simple steps and refine the things that make you feel better. You don't have to be doing something special during your recovery in the belief that you should be making up for lost time. Little things keep us well. Small, sensory pleasures, which bring momentary joy. Train the eye to spot each passing delight, a butterfly warming its wings, a swift's acrobatic flight, or dew held in a spider's web. Their cumulative effect will reinforce the precious feeling that you are doing okay.

7. Happiness is simple

Dutch sociology professor Ruut Veenhoven asked eight thousand people in one hundred and forty countries to rate how satisfied they were with their lives on a scale of one to ten. He then collated the figures to create a World Database of Happiness. Veenhoven found that happiness does not increase significantly once basic material needs, such as a steady income and a roof over our head, have been met. Further material gain, such as a bigger car, a palatial house, more status, or a fat pay rise does not guarantee more happiness, despite what we might believe. Political scientist Robert Lane argues that the culture of aspiration in Western society has made us more miserable. Over the past two generations, rates of clinical depression have doubled. We spend too much time trying to keep up with the Jones's, yet the Jones's aren't happy either. Happiness isn't found in the glove compartment of a new car, or the hem of an expensive dress. Happiness is subtler than that. It comes with an acceptance that life is messy and absurd, with moments of clarity along the way. Try and break the cycle of want and feel good about where you are right now. Chances are, life isn't be much better anywhere else.

Economist Andrew Oswald believes that happiness resembles a U-curve. His research suggests we tend to be satisfied with life in our early twenties. We become less satisfied as we move towards middle age, reaching our lowest point around forty-two. The curve then turns upward, as long as we stay healthy. We become more satisfied, with those in their sixties apparently expressing the highest satisfaction of all.

8. Rise like a phoenix

Achievement will often rise from the ashes of failure and disappointment if you learn from your experiences. Drug smuggler Sandra Gregory spent five years in a Bangkok jail then went to Oxford University and rebuilt the life she had thrown away. German author Hermann Hesse (1877-1962) spent time in his early life contemplating suicide. He articulated his struggle for meaning and inspired a generation, receiving the Nobel Prize for Literature in 1946.

Mental breakdowns give you an opportunity to think about the life you want to lead. Finding that illusive sense of purpose means reaching out and relating to concepts that are bigger, more enduring and more significant than you. Religion and spirituality offer higher meaning but you need not take this path. Ask yourself what you want your life to be about. You can infuse meaning into your life in various ways. You may choose to be kind, to help others, to make people laugh.

9. Drive yourself to distraction

Philosopher John Stuart Mill recovered from acute depression after he read a moving story, which made him forget about his depression. Mill recognised that happiness was a paradox. "Ask yourself whether you are happy and you cease to be so," he wrote. Mill believed that happy people fixed their mind on things outside themselves, "on the happiness of others, on the improvement of mankind, even on some art or pursuit." Dr Mihaly Csikszentmihalyi describes the process of completely absorbing oneself in an activity as 'flow'. Find what makes you flow.

10. Search for acceptance

Accepting who you are is the hardest part of your recovery. It is also the most liberating. Once you have accepted that mental distress has been part of your life, you can overcome it. Daphne du Maurier's *I'll Never Be Young Again* features a character who recovers from suicidal depression. In a moving passage, he says: "I am happier now than I have ever been. The restlessness has gone, the indecision and also the great heights of exultation and the strange depths of desolation. I am secure now and certain of myself. There is peace and contentment." Acceptance means balancing sorrow felt for opportunities lost with joy for good choices made.

Simon Heyes

"To dare is to lose one's footing momentarily. To not dare is to lose oneself."

Soren Kierkegaard

Relapse

"Courage does not always roar. Sometimes courage is the quiet voice at the end of day saying I will try again tomorrow."

Mary Allen Radmacher

Your road to recovery is likely to be bumpy. Unexpected setbacks will knock you off course but it is important not to over react when they do. If you start to slip backwards, don't panic. A relapse is rarely as big as it seems. Try and reflect on why things have gone wrong because there is usually a logical reason. Changing habits, especially negative ones, requires perseverance. Always remember that two steps forward and one step back is still progress in the right direction.

I had to face various setbacks during my recovery, which knocked my confidence, but I learned to rise above it. I told myself that I wasn't abnormal. Confidence is crucial in dealing with a relapse. Believe that you can overcome whatever the world throws at you. A mistake doesn't equal failure. A mistakes is an opportunity to learn. With each mistake, you learn a little more, until finally, you can join the world again.

Case History

Jenny Baxani was diagnosed with nervous exhaustion when she was a teenager following a long illness. Since then, the mental health service has changed her diagnosis twice. She has also had to cope with the suicide of her father. She is an artist and runs regular workshops for people with mental health problems called Positive Images. She is sixty-one and lives in Devon. She has two children and four grand-children.

"I first became unwell after a period in hospital. A toe infection developed into gangrene and I thought I was going to lose my leg. I was seventeen. But the operation was successful and I was sent to a convalescent home. I didn't like it there. I wanted to get away and be on my own but I couldn't. I was also addicted to sleeping pills. Everything became too much and I was diagnosed with nervous exhaustion. My diagnosis was later changed to manic depression, then bi-polar disturbance.

I live on my own and try to keep busy. I have a little dog who gives me companionship and makes me take regular exercise. My artwork has really helped maintain my recovery. A recent trip to China had a profound effect. I was so eager to take it all in. I loved the culture, the art, the people. I bought painting brushes and have started using them in my work. It was such an absorbing trip. It made me forget about my illness. I also love music and gardening. I moved to North Devon to be closer to my family. Grand-children are so therapeutic. They demand you join their world and lose yourself in play. They talk about things like everlasting life and I feel my spirit continuing in them after I've gone.

In the past five years, I've had three dips, which lasted two or three weeks. I've learned to spot the warning signs. I am not myself, I want to stay in bed, I don't want to cook. That's when I know it's time to call my psychiatric nurse, who comes to see me within twenty-four hours. I know I would slip further without his support. He tells me to stick to my normal routine. It's not always what I want to hear but I trust his judgment. It puts me right again. My life returns and I am back in control. Once you have learned to spot the signs of a relapse early, your battle with mental illness is almost won.

I try not to bother my family because they know my past and tend to panic. I have never felt ashamed of my condition. I take medication because something is missing in my body like someone with angina takes medication for their heart. I learned the hard way, though. A few times, I thought I was better and flushed my pills down the toilet. On each occasion, I was sectioned within a fortnight."

Jenny Baxani

Relapse tips

1. Turn dips into blips

Recovery is rarely smooth. Setbacks will occur. The trick is not to blame yourself. One failure does not mean you will fail every time. Suppose you admire someone from a distance but cannot pluck up the courage to talk to them. Rather than convince yourself that you will always feel shy in similar situations, tell yourself that you will feel more confident next time. Look for the hidden net gains that could prevent the same situation occurring again. Learn from the experience and continue to plan for the future. Adopting a positive approach to failure reduces the likelihood of a relapse developing into a breakdown.

2. Form fluctuates but recovery can be permanent

Sporting greats can grind out a performance when their form dips because they are confident that their form will return. You may have days when you feel lonely, anxious and depressed. That does not mean you are on the verge of a relapse. We all have bad days. It is part of being human. When they materialise, try and think about someone you respect and care about. How would they react in the same situation? Keep things in perspective and let the mood pass. Rest assured, it will.

3. Nip it in the bud

A relapse is likely to occur under certain conditions. These vary from person to person. Learning what conditions trigger you off is a key component in making a successful recovery. Once you have trained yourself to spot the early warning signs, you can take preventative action. Common triggers are stress, boredom, strained relationships, loneliness, anniversaries, even full moons. Early warning signs include erratic sleeping patterns, drinking too much alcohol and mulling over the past. Your Wellness Recovery Action Plan (see Creative tips) comes to the fore here. With a plan of action thought out and written down in advance, you will be better equipped to halt the slide before you go into freefall.

4. Switch off

Remember there is more to life than mental health. In *On and Off the Field*, cricketer Ed Smith describes the trials and tribulations of surviving a cricket season. Being able to switch off stopped him "going mad". The lesson is universal. It is exhausting if you are constantly thinking about how you are doing in life. Switch off and let your mind be.

5. Positives attract

In the event of a relapse, avoid the temptation to wallow. When things go wrong, I know from experience it is easy to literally hide beneath the blanket and close the door to the world. Slipping into victim mode is an easy option. Old negative thoughts can quickly return. The key is to realise that these are only thoughts and you don't need to act on them. You have a choice now. Exercise it with vigour. Learn a way out of the labyrinth and move on.

Positive Role Model Abraham Lincoln lost his mother when he was nine years old and suffered a breakdown after a close friend died when he was thirty-four. He went on to become US President at the age of fifty-two.

"We ask ourselves, who am I to be brilliant, gorgeous, talented and fabulous? Actually, who are you not to be? Your playing small does not serve the world. There is nothing enlightened about shrinking so that other people won't feel insecure around you. And as we let our own light shine we consciously give other people permission to do the same. As we are liberated from our own fear, our presence automatically liberates others."

Nelson Mandela

So how am I today? I still struggle with depression and panic attacks but I live a relatively normal life. My experience has taught me that recovery starts when we hit rock bottom. From there we can rebuild our lives on stronger foundations. I am no longer embarrassed about my mental condition. In the past, I wasted a lot of energy keeping it hidden. Now I see my breakdowns in a different light. They forced me to change. I congratulate myself on achieving what I do in spite of my mental state. I try to count my blessings and make the most of my life.

In the past, people with mental distress were said to be possessed by the devil. Today, it would be more accurate to say we feel dispossessed, alienated from our true selves. Recovery is about possessing that true self again.

We should not feel ashamed about who we are and what we have been through. Recovery is realising that we are not abnormal; that we are in good company. Our individual accounts of mental collapse are not isolated events but hint at common concerns in an age of collective insecurity. Recognising the shared patterns in our mental breakdowns could help forge a renewed spirit of community and reduce our isolation and loneliness.

I have no blueprint to offer. Neither have I tried to muddle you with magic formulas. This guide is about facing up to where you are in life, deciding what recovery means for you and inspiring change to achieve it. As we recover we learn to accept that some suffering is good for us; our successes would have little meaning without it. There is no finishing line to say you have recovered. Recovery has no finite end. It is ongoing and needs nurturing.

Good luck!

Simon Heyes

"I cannot imagine becoming jaded to life."
Dr. Kay Redfield Jamison

Selected bibliography

Cantopher, T., *Depressive Illness: The curse of the strong*, Sheldon Press, 2003

Copeland, M., *Wellness Recovery Action Plan*, Peach Press, 2001

De Botton, A., *Status Anxiety*, Hamish Hamilton, 2004

Du Maurier, D., *I'll Never Be Young Again*, Arrow, 1994

Griffiths, T., *Lost and Then Found*, Paternoster Press, 2002

Groopman, J., *The Anatomy of Hope*, Random House, 2004

Hess, H., *The Prodigy*, Penguin, 1973

Kubler Ross, E., *On Death and Dying*, Scribner, 1997

Lott, T., *The Scent of Dried Roses*, Penguin, 1996

Mill, J.S., *Autobiography*, Penguin, 1989

O'Hanlon, B., *Thriving Through Crisis*, Perigee Books, 2004

Redfield Jamison, K., *An Unquiet Mind*, Vintage Books, 1996

Scott Peck, M., *The Road Less Travelled*, Rider, 1988

Solomon, A., *The Noonday Demon*, Scribner, 2001

Storr, A., *Churchill's Black Dog, Kafka's Mice, and Other Phenomena of the Human Mind*, Grove Press, 1988

Styron, W., *Darkness Visible*, Random House, 1990

Tolstoy, L., *A Confession*, Penguin, 1987

Zola, E., *Geminal*, Oxford University Press, 1998